Publishing history

First Edition April 2012

Acknowledgements

To Lisa and Tara for helping me put the work together. To the Great Spirit and to my children for being who they are!

Introduction

These stories and channelled pieces are an attempt to help us look at the journey of the soul and the mind in different ways and in so doing hopefully they will lead us to amore love based life.

My advice to you the reader, is don't take anything too serious, you will be aware on a deep level what is meant for you in the book.

But remember I believe there is no such thing as coincidence, and you are reading this book.

Index

Creation at our Fingertips

You are at the point of creation; you shape it, energise it and maintain it. Your thoughts and actions are the Architects and constructors of creation.

When you change yourself, you change the world. The world is but a divine mirror that helps you see all aspects of personality. The aim of the physical is to accept and love all aspects of yourself, the reflections help you.

I the creator work through everyone and everything. I energise you and you energise change. I dream and you experience.

When I say you I mean the part of you that deals with the illusion of being separate. Your mind creates and examines the illusion of duality which was created to enables choice that leads to the experience of uniqueness, contrast and free will.

Your mind has been gifted with magnetic qualities to draw in the experience your mind focuses on. The clearer the focus of the mind the stronger the magnetism it can generate.

Your mind will be influenced in the duality by one of the two energies that help create the contrast.

These energies are vital and directly effect and shape your world view.

The more you are affected by either of the energies the stronger your world view will become.

The energies are love experiencing infinite possibilities this is what some people call their higher self and searching safety but fearing loss which some people call the lower mind. I short if you identify with either love or fear your choices will have a profound effect on the type of experiences you experience.

Your mind is like a filter that will maintain your connection with your selected energy. It will draw in supporting experiences to confirm your beliefs and weaken your receptiveness to other experiences.

Over the years your mind is strengthened or weakened in its ability to attract experiences and your awareness of your mind filter is vital to improving attraction.

You need to view your mind filter setting in relationship to the life you would choose, if the match and are aligned then reinforce the filter if not clean the filter.

Be at one with life and live in the present, trust that you are supported and loved, after the entire universe is designed to interact and respond with your thoughts and actions. Set clear goals to help you clear your filter and set it to attract.

Finger Nails

To help you understand the relationship between you and myself I will use the example of your finger nails. If you look at them they appear different from your hand and yet they are made from the same thing.

If you imagine the nail as yourself and the finger as your soul, you can begin to understand the human relationship with myself.

If the nail was to view the world from as open hand it would see everybody and everything as different and separate, yet it would realise it is connected to myself and all that is.

If you could imagine that your finger represents your soul, this supports you to experience whatever your mind decides, however because of the placement of the nail on the finger it can only move with the help of the finger (soul) and the soul is restricted by the movement of the hand (the soul group) which in turn is restricted by the arm (the human consciousness) this is connected to the body (the mass consciousness).

I am at the heart of this consciousness and my heart pumps the blood of consciousness and awareness through all things.

I have used the term mass consciousness because 'mass or matter' has its own rules and consciousness designed to experience limitation.

Time, space, gravity and electromagnetism help confine all things in their energy blue print. This is an illusion, and separation, death and duality are all part of it. We are all one.

If I can now return to the concept of the nail, it is impossible to do anything against my will and you agreed to the limitation before you arrived on Earth.

If you look outwards you will constantly feel alone and unconnected but when you look within you will remember your divine origin and your connectedness to all that is.

All I ask of you is to remember you are loved and we are one.

You are all my children, and as a parent I love all my children whether they are playing out without a thought about me or sat communicating with me.

If any of my children call to me I will always listen and respond.

The Seed and the Light

If you imagine that we are all seeds planted deep into the seeds planted deep into the darkness of the Earth's soil. We have an inbuilt desire and ability to find the light that nurtures our growth and keeps us healthy. Simply we trust and grow to the light and prosper.

Then all of a sudden we begin to see lots of less bright lights all over the place and we begin to wonder which light to follow, as the other lesser lights to join up and begin to call some to us we are the light of reason, you will not be alone with us, we are the only light you need. You begin to wonder if this was the light you were sending, yet a part of us still feels the pull to the lights you have the inbuilt connection too.

The Water Wheel of Life

If you view your life as a water wheel, it can appear that there are times when you are weighted down by problems or pain.

This is like the water entering the first chamber of the water wheel. Then if you cannot cope with the flow of the problem it pours into the next chamber of the water wheel. If you cannot cope with the flow of problems it pours into the next chamber and the next until the wheel begins to turn.

When the wheel is working fully it will be half full of water and half the chambers will be empty. This helps to generate the energy of choice and you can decide to view the wheel as either half empty or half full.

If you are secure in the centre of the half full view you will be aware of the water and the movement but remain confident and dry. Believing you will always get through each problem you have.

If you get stuck in the centre of the water you will always feel like you're drowning and it will never end.

Use the energy of choice the wheel generates to decide which you prefer.

The Light Bulb

One day in a large office there were a number of light bulbs, each unique and individual, some had a shadow on them and some were shaded different colours. When the room became darker an energy would light up the bulbs and they became aware of each other and everything, then the energy would return to its source and the bulbs would sleep.

This happened for a few nights and then they began to talk to each other, or the energy within them did, 'Wow its great being a light bulb' one said happily 'yes' agreed another, they look around the room and saw all the different things and recognised the same energy in all of them.

That night the light bulbs did not sleep as well, they had been disturbed by the energy and they talked amongst themselves. 'I don't understand the energy in all things, surly light bulbs are most important and we give light to everything' one bulb said 'yes we do, the toaster could not be seen all the time without us' another bulb commented in agreement.

The next day the energy again animated the bulb and wonder of the marvels of the kitchen. This became the norm each day the energy animated the bulb and by night the bulbs were discussing their place and importance in the kitchen.

One day there was a bang and a bulb stopped producing light, it could no longer talk to the other bulbs or do anything.

That night the bulbs talked about the energy that worked the bulb that had helped it talk and shine. Some felt it had disappeared and would never return again, another believed it would return as a bulb, others thought if the bulb was not good when it was alive the energy may come back as a toaster.

One light bulb decided to ask the energy when it lit him up. The next day he asked the energy and he was surprised by the answer, the energy said 'some energy does indeed return to the source and stays there, some energy will come back as a light bulb to experience that again, some energy may come back as a toaster or other things but not as a punishment but to experience something different', that night the light bulb; now fully awake wants to tell the others what the energy had told him, some listened and became more awake others drifted in and out of sleep while lots and lots shouted be quiet and go back to sleep. The bulb decided to whisper his truth to all who wanted to listen as he did those who did not; he whispered his truth 'ask the energy'.

The Divine Mirror

We are all one, everything you see in the world is a reflection of you. You are all a reflection of me, so you are all divine. So why is there so much shadow in the reflections you may see?

I will tell you, as a body is born their mirror is perfectly clear, they reflect my total glory. They are trusting, loving and offering themselves in perfect services to myself. They are willing and openly offer themselves to whatever experiences come their way, they are connected to the knowledge that they have entered the illusion of duality and that the expansion of consciousness is sole purpose. They know that they are spirit having a human experience.

Then they begin to pick up the fears of people around them, each one leaves a shadow on the mirror and in the filter. They are taught that acceptance is love and acceptance can be with held. So love is not guaranteed always and forever, you can allow you mind to distraught it or to believe you can deny it. The nature of love is constant and unwavering. The human experience can be one of pure love and joy, with your inner knowing and love reflecting out to everyone around and theirs reflecting to you or your fears can cloud your mirror and block your light from reflecting and the shadow is reflected back to you by others.

Free Choice

To experience the illusion of separation you have been given unique and amazing minds.

The minds role is to process information it receives and then to form an opinion of who you are and supply experiences to support this view.

To create the illusion the mind is given the opinion of everyone being and things being separate. The mind then works to see what makes everyone different while the soul works to show what unifies everything.

The mind develops a character for you to play throughout the physical life in the divine drama. The character in conjunction with the mind works through a number of scripts and either accepts or rejects them on an ongoing basis.

Then the mind energetically draws the experiences to you. If you believe life is painful and pointless, evidence and experience will be drawn to confirm just that. Likewise if you believe it is wonderful.

You have free choice to change your views and experiences at any time. If we can recall the idea of the finger nail the soul has been placed in an environment that will draw certain experiences but then it can move to others.

You can become your own script writer or never throw off your childhood scripts given to you before you could understand what you felt about the world.

For choice to exist, you needed very different experiences, some you may feel desirable, some not so enjoyable.

Some bring people together others push them apart. Some help all and some help a few and can cause difficulties to others. Some views you take can elevate people above anything else, this can lead to other beings falling foul to your choices.

Your mind with the help of your soul has tried to order the illusion into positive and negative experiences and actions. It is still an illusion but this helps the divine drama.

Love and Fear

Within the illusion of your reality there are two emotions at the core of thought and action.

Love experiencing infinite possibilities in the emotion that best describes the function of the soul within the world. Growth and change is the desired aim of the soul as this is in line with the constantly evolving consciousness that is within all of us.

All experiences whether perceived as a joyful or painful are important to the evolution of consciousness and essential for growth.

The energy of thought fuels so much growth and emotion (energy in motion) the tell tale sign of the love energy is enthusiasm and urgency, this is to help you push through the negative filter and engage life. The negative emotion is searching safely but fearing loss.

This energy works for the mind and is involved in creating the illusion of a never changing world and the fear of anything or body different than you may have experienced. The mind may hold on to a negative past experience or negative information to reinforce its position within the energy.

The love energy filter sees life as a labyrinth where it is impossible to be lost or lose connection to the centre of all that is. Nothing can be wrong it just appears to be going away from the centre but it is always connected and will always find the way.

The fear filter sees life as a maze designed to trick you and lead you astray so you end up abandoned and lost, leaving you totally alone and afraid with no hope or support.

In either mind set your mind will try to produce evidence of your beliefs. So I ask you, which world do you want to create?

The Captain of the Ship

One day a man was born and was given the control and responsibility to sail a ship safely through the ocean of live. Everybody looks to him to see what to do, he is all important and all powerful. He spends years working hard making sure that he does his best keeping the things moving and making the best of things.

He now is totally in control and even instructions from his employers were now greeted disapproval. He no longer values anyone's opinions other than his own.

Then the captain received a message that this was his last journey, the ship was being retired and no longer needed. He was shocked, sad, angry, uncertain and afraid. He felt anything but the in control captain he had been most of his life.

He decided to not tell the crew of the owner's plans and pretend nothing was happening that everything was normal. One day a crew member asked him about the rumours of the ship being retired at the end of the journey, the captain asked why they would retire this wonderful ship; don't believe all that nonsense you hear said the captain.

The captain became more afraid, what would he do? What would happen to him? Surely he was important to be retired and the ship to be recycled.

Your mind is the captain of your ship, he will sometimes resist your soul (the owner) of your ship. He may become fear filled and reflect all suggestions that he is not more important than he feels he is. The idea of life continuing without him in control scares him totally.

Fighting your mind will only scare him more, don't think, trust your inner voice and have no desire to convince others or even your mind. There is a knowing that comes from being centred in the heart, mind and the now. The mind lives in the past of whom it was or the future of who it will be. The mind cannot live in the moment for it feels redundant. Don't forget only fear needs evidence that does not support its world view.

The Filter

The mind has become the filter for your reality; it seeks out and attracts experiences that confirm its beliefs.

So your mind could have decided that the world is not safe, your mind will begin to look for evidence from the television, newspapers. Other peoples experiences or its own memory. With each piece of evidence the mind collects, it begins to build up a castle to protect itself, thought by thought, stone by stone. Soon the castle becomes a prison with you feeling unable to venture out of its walls, here you are now trapped in the fear vibration, the filter is very important with the law of attraction.

The captain of the ships always sees things from his own perspective, so do most humans, they try to see a human having a spiritual experience not a spirit having a human experience.

This can lead to so much wisdom and experience being untapped by them. They trowel the well trodden paths of the human scripts, most of which lead to the low fear based energy and then experiencing themselves through pain. The spirit allows this because one day they will wake up and remember the loving parent who will then remind the person of their own great power and strength they have.

The brain can develop a filter of fear, which leads to the person deciding against actions because they can no longer see what they can gain from the actions, or the fear of the pain the action might invoke.

Instead of the selfish act of services which brings an instant reward when done lovingly, for you cannot give without receiving. Your mind may try to reflect this by saying, how can this work? If I give away money, how will I get it back?

Let me suggest that if you want something enough then you will always find a way to do it. How many people find a way to do something for a child or loved one they would normally find difficult or impossible for themselves?

The Magic Mirror

Once upon a time on a sunny afternoon a little girl sat crying in her garden. She was thinking about all the nasty names people at School had called her. Then through the tears she saw something shining in a spider's web. The little girl stopped crying and began to focus on the bright light in the web. To her amazement and surprise it was a beautiful fairy with her leg stuck in the web.

"Help me please" begged the fairy.

The little girl carefully moved the web from the fairies leg and released her. The fairy then flew away, but before she did the fairy thanked the little girl and told her how beautiful she was. The little girl told the fairy that she did not feel beautiful and indeed she felt horrible and not nice at all.

The fairy stopped and thought about how she could help the little girl.

"I know I will give you a present to help you remember you are beautiful" the fairy told her.

"What? What?" asked the little girl excitedly.

The fairy said no more and shook her magic wand. With a rainbow coloured flash a mirror appeared, but this was no ordinary mirror this one was magic.

"That's lovely!" said the little girl in mixture of excitement and wonder.

"It's not only beautiful it is magic as well" the fairy told her.

"Why, what does it do?" asked the girl almost unable to control her excitement.

"It shows how truly beautiful you are when you look in it" the fairy told her with a beaming smile.

The little girl moved slowly to the mirror almost afraid of what she may see, bravely she looked in the mirror and her eyes filled with tears.

"What's the matter?" asked the fairy concerned.

"I am so beautiful "yelled the little girl unable to stop the joy and relief pouring out of her.

"That's amazing I will never feel ugly again". She promised with a smile and thanked the fairy for the wonderful gift. In turn the fairy thanked the little girl and disappeared.

The next day at School the little girl was playing by herself, when the bullies came over and began their normal nasty ways. First they called her horrible names, this would normally make her cry but today she remembered the magic mirror and how beautiful she was. This made the bullies angry and they pushed her to see if she would cry, they shouted so loud a teacher heard and moved them away, the little girl could hear the teacher telling the bullies that they would have to stay behind after School. After School the bullies talked about how the little girl had changed and how they would get their revenge when the teacher was not there.

The following day the little girl went to School and again the bullies called her nasty names, and again the little girl remember she was beautiful, she became strong.

Day after day this happened until one bully asked "Why don't you get upset anymore when we call you names?"

The little girl replied with a smile "I have a magic mirror at home that tells me how beautiful I am and that your nasty names are not true, so you won't upset me anymore".

The other children in the play ground had seen the little girl stand up to the bullies and this had given them courage to do the same.

The bullies became really concerned that people would not be scared of them anymore. They had to upset the little girl again but how? They decided to break the magic mirror. That night they followed the little girl home. They watched her go into the house and stand in front of the mirror they saw her smile to herself and leave the room to play in the garden.

The bullies quietly sneaked into the house. They slowly moved over to the mirror.

"This mirror doesn't work, it's all cloudy" one bully said angrily.

Another bully pulled a large stone from his pocket and shouted "This will teach her!" throwing the stone at the mirror.

The stone crashed into the middle of the mirror. The bullies waited for the sound and pieces of breaking glass to fill the room. But the only noise they heard was the stone hitting the floor. The smiles on the faces of the bullies soon disappeared and were replaced with a stunned look.

"Maybe it is magic!" one said panicking.

"Let's colour it and make it so she can't see herself in it!" said another bully trying not to look afraid.

Quickly they all began to put different colours on the mirror. Now when the little girl would look in the mirror she would always see what they had done and not her beauty. After they had finished they hid outside so they could see her face when she looked in the mirror.

The little girl came in from the garden unaware of what had just happened. She was too happy in the garden to worry about anything. The garden had become a place of wonder and magic since the fairies visit.

She moved across to the mirror to look at her reflection. This she did every night partly to remind her about the fairy and partly to remind her she was not all the nasty things the bullies said. But tonight was going to be very different and nothing had prepared her for it. She looked in the mirror and let out a scream, her tears flowed freely, "That's not me!" she sobbed.

The bullies walked away laughing and pleased they had hurt her again.

The little girl took the mirror into her attic and left it there not wanting to see it or the fairy again.

The next day at School the bullies attacked her with horrible names again and the girl cried and cried. The other children saw her cry and their courage disappeared as well. This carried on for the most of the little girls School life until the bullies were expelled or their families moved away. Even then the girl felt really bad.

One day she heard about a wise woman from a distant village who could help. She decided to go and see her and tell her about the mirror. The journey was long and she wondered if the wise woman would believe her about the fairy and the magic mirror. When she arrived the girl told her everything about the fairy and the mirror and how it turned out to be a curse. The wise woman corrected her, nothing given from the heart is a curse. She then told the girl how to clean the mirror. The girl thanked her and walked home.

"Is this really going to work?" she asked herself.

As she got home she ran up to the attic and brought the mirror down stairs. Half in hope and half in fear she cleaned the mirror, and to her amazement she could see it clearing until she was looking at her beautiful reflection again in the mirror.

The girl grabbed her coat and ran to the wise woman's village to thank her. She felt young and happy again for the first time in years. She finally arrived and thanked the wise woman and started home.

On the way home she started to think about the nasty bullies who had made her life terrible. She became angrier and angrier. When she got in she walked across to the mirror and was shocked to see it cloudy. She tried cleaning it again but it did not help. She panicked and decided to go to the wise woman again. This time she was really tired and it was raining.

Finally she arrived at the wise woman's house and told her what had happened. The wise woman asked her if she had bad thoughts about anyone. The girl told her the truth and the wise woman said "If you walk home and keep saying I love you, I'm sorry, please forgive me your mirror will clear."

The wet and tired girl began to walk home in the rain. "Why should I forgive them when I'm not sorry? How could I love them? No I won't do it!"

She carried on in the rain and then thought "Why don't I forgive them they are not important now only my happiness, maybe I need to do this to forget them!"

The girl started to say what the wise woman told her. She began to feel better "That's strange!" she thought.

Then as she got nearer home the sun came out and a huge beautiful rainbow came out. The rainbow looked like it ended near her house.

She began to hurry, still saying the words the wise woman had given her. When she arrived she could see the rainbow ended in her front garden. She ran the last part of the journey home excited and happy. She ran into the garden and danced in the beautiful rainbow light.

After a while she remembered the mirror and went in the house to look at it. Yet again tears filled her eyes she appeared even more beautiful with the rainbow colours behind her, but even more amazingly she could see the beautiful fairy on her shoulder.

"Did you think I would forget you?" the fairy asked with a smile.

The Tree that Lost its Roots

Once upon a time a tree lived with all his brothers and sisters in a beautiful garden. He felt at one with them all; the earth his mother, the sun his father and the great spirits love that was within them all.

His days were simply beautiful; he reached to the sun with his branches of bright green leaves whilst hugging the earth with his curling roots of solid oak. When the clouds came, the rain dripped one rain drop at a time on his green leaves and into the soil around his broad trunk giving refreshment and the gift of life, as he sucked up the precious gift he thanked the clouds.

When the wind blew he would bow to it, for it was the wind that would carry and spread his seeds and place them where they were meant to be. Each moment was filled with beauty.

The Tree became bored and asked "Why do I have to grow to the light every day?"

"I don't know!" said a young tree "I guess I do it because my parents do it!"

Then the older Tree told him that it was "To thank the Sun for its part in the gift of life!"

He mocked the old tree "You old fool; the sun will shine even if we don't reach up to it!"

The old tree just reached for the Sun with his long branches of green leaves, which upset the rude young tree.

"You will never reach the sun, your life is to bow to the wind, praise the Sun and give all to the Earth! What fools!" he said now in an angry mood.

The old tree reached higher to the Sun and felt the warmth and bliss.

The angry tree then noticed for the first time that all the trees and animals in the garden were different and unique.

"Which are the best trees or animals?" he asked. The old tree told him that each is wonderful in their own way and the garden was more beautiful for each of them.

The angry tree did not like that answer and decided that he was the most special and made fun of some other trees and animals, he would not share or be friendly with them.

The old tree tried to warn him. "The things you do and say will grow into your leaves and fruit and when they fall from you they will feed you!"

The angry tree said "Be quiet you old fool, I am better than all of you!"

"My friend the great spirit created us all equally!" the old tree replied while reaching for the Sun.

"Fool!" shouted the angry Tree. "There is no Great Spirit!"

"How did we get here then?" asked the little tree a little afraid.

"From a seed!" replied the angry tree.

"But that must come from a tree! Where did that seed come from?" Asked the little tree confused.

"I think we must have started out as something else then changed into trees!" the angry tree said unsure now himself.

"What?" question the little tree.

"I don't know for sure" said the angry tree sheepishly.

"But you are sure there is no Great Spirit?" asked the old tree.

"I will prove you can change, I will no longer reach for the Sun nor will I dig as deep into mother Earth to share with her!" he said loudly. This will show everyone I am right.

"If you don't grow your roots into the ground the wind will blow you over and you will not grow!" said the little tree concerned.

"I will change; I will split my trunk into two and use branches on the ends of them for extra grip." He said.

Over the years he did indeed change his shape, and he did become less and less like a tree.

When the wind came to move all the seeds to where they needed to go. The angry tree had already dropped his fruit because it was so bitter.

The wind blew really hard and the angry tree was not going to bend. All his leaves blew off then one by one all his branches blew away until it only had two left. He then decided to bend.

When the wind stopped the angry tree decided to pull up his roots and walk out of the garden.

"Where are you going?" the old tree asked.

"I am going where the wind doesn't blow!" said the angry tree.

"There is nowhere that you can be untouched by the Great Spirit!" the old tree said calmly while reaching for the Sun.

"Trees are stupid! From now on I am going to be called a man!"

Man left the beautiful garden and entered the valley where true to his word for many years he lived in a cave away from the wind.

That is why man are always seeking roots and to belong. Some men still cannot see their part in the Great Spirits plans. The seed of love that the Great Spirit planted in the first tree to connect it to all things is still in every person!

www.ingramcontent.com/pod-product-compliance
Lightning Source LLC
LaVergne TN
LVHW051712080426
835511LV00017B/2867